MW01131090

Searchlight BOOKS™

Hunting and Fishing

Bowhunting

Kyle Brach

Lerner Publications ◆ Minneapolis

Lerner Publications Company
An imprint of Lerner Publishing Group, Inc.
241 First Avenue North
Minneapolis, MN 55401 USA

For reading levels and more information, look up this title at www.lernerbooks.com.

Main body text set in Adrianna Regular.
Typeface provided by Chank.

Library of Congress Cataloging-in-Publication Data

Names: Brach, Kyle, author.
Title: Bowhunting / Kyle Brach.
Description: Minneapolis : Lerner Publications , [2024] | Series: Searchlight books - hunting and fishing | Includes bibliographical references and index. | Audience: Ages 8–11 | Audience: Grades 4–6 | Summary: "Hunting game with a bow and arrow, or bowhunting, has been around for thousands of years. Readers will love learning about the basics of bowhunting, how to stay safe while hunting, and more"— Provided by publisher.
Identifiers: LCCN 2022038718 (print) | LCCN 2022038719 (ebook) | ISBN 9781728491547 (library binding) | ISBN 9798765603734 (paperback) | ISBN 9798765600351 (ebook)
Subjects: LCSH: Bowhunting—Juvenile literature.
Classification: LCC SK36 .R43 2024 (print) | LCC SK36 (ebook) | DDC 799.2/15—dc23/eng/20220816

LC record available at https://lccn.loc.gov/2022038718
LC ebook record available at https://lccn.loc.gov/2022038719

Manufactured in the United States of America
1–CG–7/15/23

Table of Contents

Chapter 1

GOING BOWHUNTING

You are out bowhunting in the woods when you stop in your tracks. You get very quiet and still. There's something rustling in the leaves. Slowly, you walk closer to the rustling noise. Step by silent step, you creep forward. You get in position before carefully removing an arrow from your quiver. You aim and pull the string back. With the deer in sight, you release the arrow.

BOWHUNTERS GET CLOSE TO NATURE IN THE GREAT OUTDOORS.

▼

The white-tailed deer is the most popular prey for bowhunting.

Game is any wild animal that is hunted. They are broken down into three groups: fowl, small game, and large game.

For bowhunting, fowl includes birds such as wild turkeys. Popular small game includes squirrels, foxes, and rabbits. Large game includes black bears, elk, deer, and more.

Hunting History

Thousands of years before grocery stores, humans were hunters and gatherers. They didn't have farms or ranches like we have now. But they did have bows and arrows. In fact, humans have hunted with bows and arrows since the Stone Age. Archaeologists have found sixty-thousand-year-old bone arrow points in Africa. In Spain, seven-thousand-year-old cave drawings show hunting scenes.

Most people may not need to hunt anymore. But bowhunting lets us walk in our ancestors' footsteps.

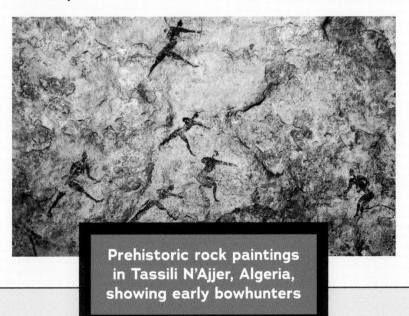

Prehistoric rock paintings in Tassili N'Ajjer, Algeria, showing early bowhunters

The Right Bow for You

A bow is a weapon made by attaching a string to a curved piece of wood or other material. There are three main types of modern bows you can use: a compound bow, longbow, and recurve bow.

Young hunters often start with a draw weight of 20 pounds (9.1 kg). A minimum of 40 pounds (18.1 kg) is needed for hunting.

A compound bow uses adjustable wheels, cables, and pulleys to make it easier to draw the string back. The longbow, a traditional-style bow, is long and straight with a handle in the middle. A recurve bow is similar to the longbow, but it curves upward at both ends.

Bows are identified by their draw weight in pounds. Draw weight is the amount of force needed to draw a bow. If a bow is rated 40 pounds (18.1 kg), it takes 40 pounds of strength to pull the string that shoots the arrow. The harder it is to pull the string, the farther the arrow will go.

A compound bow

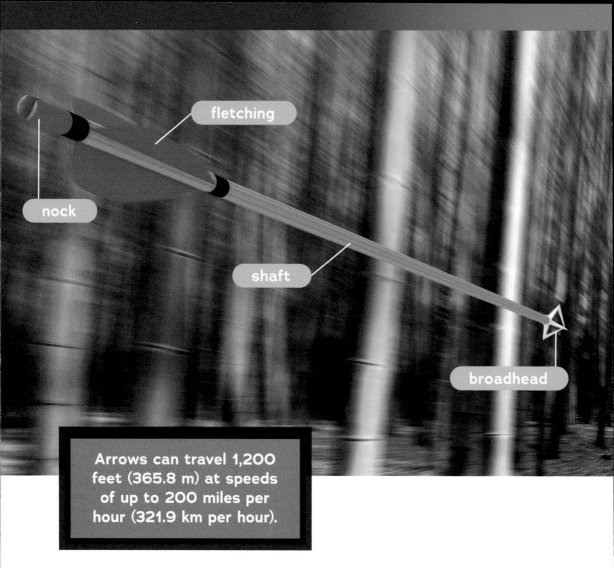

nock

fletching

shaft

broadhead

Arrows can travel 1,200 feet (365.8 m) at speeds of up to 200 miles per hour (321.9 km per hour).

Arrows

Arrows can be made from aluminum, wood, fiberglass, or graphite. The shaft is the long part of the arrow. The broadhead is the arrow's sharp point. The nock is at the other end of the shaft. It has a slit to place on the string. The feathers that help steer the arrow are the fletching.

Other Gear

Hunters also need a finger tab or a glove to protect their fingers and hand when pulling back the string. An armguard protects the arm holding the bow. Hunters carry a container to hold arrows on their hips or backs. This is called a quiver. They also attach a sight to the bow to help improve aim.

A quiver holding arrows

Dress for Success

Hunters spend a lot of time outside. They need to be prepared for quickly changing weather. A good rule of thumb is to dress in layers. That way hunters are ready for anything.

Camouflage clothing helps hunters blend into the surroundings, making it less likely an animal will spot them.

Camouflage face paint
helps cover faces
and necks.

Clothes should be comfortable and fit well. Tight clothes make it hard to draw back the bowstring. Loose clothes get in the way. Hunters also need to wear quiet clothes. Noise from rustling clothes can scare game away. Wool, brushed cotton, and other soft fabrics are good choices. Hunting involves a lot of walking. Boots with rubber soles should fit well and be broken in.

Chapter 2

STAYING SAFE

Bows and arrows are weapons. They can be dangerous if not used correctly. To be safe, you need to know three things: how to use your bow, how to hunt safely, and how to follow hunting rules.

Practice, Practice, Practice

Bowhunting isn't something you just do without preparing first. You need a lot of archery practice. Archery is the sport of using a bow and arrow to hit a target.

You can learn from an experienced family member or a trusted adult. You can also sign up for lessons at a local archery range. Learning from a pro helps you develop good habits and skills.

When practicing archery use big targets with proper backing—and adult supervision.

Wearing an orange vest keeps other hunters from mistaking you for prey.

Bowhunting Safety

You may have to take a state-approved bowhunting safety course before you can get a hunting license. Classes usually cover outdoor survival, hunting rules, safe hunting practices, and more.

To stay safe, young hunters should always hunt with an adult. Hunters of all ages should make sure that their families know exactly where they will be hunting. It is also important to always know where other members of your hunting party are.

Carry your equipment, especially the arrows, securely. Never draw an arrow until you are ready to shoot. And always be sure the arrow is pointed in a safe direction and never pointed at people. Most of all, do not shoot something if you don't know what it is.

Following hunting rules like these keeps hunters safe.

Safe hunting means being prepared.

Where Am I?

Bowhunters should know how to take care of themselves if they get lost in the wild. They should know how to start a fire and create a shelter for protection from bad weather.

Safety gear includes an extra water bottle, a whistle to signal for help, a first aid kit, matches, and a flashlight. A compass, GPS device, and map are also great tools.

STEM Spotlight

GPS devices tell you where you are. GPS stands for global positioning system. It is a network of satellites in space that track your location on Earth and send a signal to your smartphone or device. The technology has gotten so good that some GPS devices can tell your location within 0.5 inches (1.27 cm)! They can be lifesavers if you are ever lost in the woods.

A GPS device is essential gear for bowhunters.

Chapter 3

LEARNING THE BASICS

It takes skill, knowledge, and patience to become a good bowhunter. Once you are old enough, know the hunting rules, and are skilled at archery, you can start hunting.

Bowhunting Season

In many places, bowhunting season is longer than rifle-hunting season. Each US state has its own laws.

Bowhunters need to get permission to hunt on private land. They can look online for hunting areas in their state.

Generally, bowhunting season starts in the fall and ends either in late fall or midwinter. Hunting outside of hunting season is illegal. Illegal hunting is called poaching.

In order to hunt, you need a special permit or license. Some states also make you buy a tag for each animal you plan on hunting. This helps officials keep track of how many animals are being hunted.

On the Hunt

There are two different ways you can improve your chances of finding game. One way to find game is to wait for it. Many bowhunters use a blind to hide so game can't see or smell them. A blind can be natural like boulders, bushes, or grass clumps. You can also hide in a cloth tent-like structure.

Still hunting is another hunting method that involves slowly and stealthily looking for game. As you search, it helps to think about the game you are trying to find.

Deer eat corn, soybeans, and wheat and sometimes hang out at the edges of farm fields.

For example, where does the animal you are hunting like to eat and find water? What do its footprints and scat (poop) look like? When you see the animal you are hunting, stalk it by moving quietly and slowly until you are close enough to shoot.

Hunters look for clues like these footprints to track game.

Hunters may mask their scent with skunk urine or another natural scent.

You Stink!

Many animals have an amazing sense of smell. A deer can smell sixty times better than you. If they smell you, they're gone. That's why it's always important to have the wind in your face when stalking game. That way your scent blows behind you and away from game.

Another way to hide your smell is to apply natural scents to your body, such as pine, acorns, apples, and even fox or skunk urine. You can also buy special hunting clothing or sprays that reduce body odor. Wearing rubber boots helps disguise foot odor. There's even gum to mask bad breath and make it smell less "human" to game.

Rubber-soled boots help quiet a hunter's noise and scent.

Chapter 4

RESPECTING NATURE

Bowhunting is a way to enjoy a day in the great outdoors and take time away from screens, chores, schoolwork, and noise. Enjoying nature comes with a duty to take care of it. Bowhunters do that by following the rules. They pay for licenses and tags that are required by law. They respect hunting limits and seasons.

Hunt by the Numbers

Hunters must purchase a license or permit every hunting season. The license includes the type of game and the number of animals the license holder can hunt. When hunters don't overhunt, they protect animals from extinction.

If an area has a large population of one type of game, wildlife managers might issue more hunting tags. Overpopulation of a species can lead to disease, starvation, and other problems. Keeping animal populations under control is one way that hunters help balance the ecosystem. Hunting for animals you don't have tags for is poaching, and it is illegal.

The best rule to follow in nature is to leave it like you found it.

Show Me the Money

Conservation means protecting wildlife and other natural resources. Money from hunting licenses, taxes, and tags is used to fund conservation programs. Hunters spend more money to protect wildlife than any other group.

Good conservation looks to the future. It makes sure that people will be bowhunting for many years to come.

Hunting helps prevent animal overpopulation.

Hunting Hints

- Hunters often wait on tree stands—platforms hung high in a tree—for game to come near.

- Bowhunters need to be as close as 30 yards (27.4 m) to large game before shooting. Cut that distance in half for small game.

- Practice moving silently.

- Small game can be easier to find. Hunting fast squirrels and rabbits takes practice and good aim.

- Respect your fellow hunters and stay out of their way.

Glossary

archaeologist: a person who studies the distant past by digging up and studying old buildings, materials, and bones

archery: the sport or skill of shooting at targets with a bow and arrows

blind: a shelter used to hide hunters, so they remain undetected by animals

conservation: the act of preserving and protecting natural resources

draw: to pull back the string of a bow in order to shoot an arrow

ecosystem: a community or group of living organisms that live in and interact with each other in the same environment

extinction: the dying out or elimination of a species

poaching: hunting illegally

season: a period of the year associated with something (for example, hunting season)

tracking: following the footprints or other traces of an animal

Learn More

Brach, Kyle. *Deer Hunting*. Minneapolis: Lerner Books, 2024.

Britannica Kids: Archery
    https://kids.britannica.com/students/article/archery/272937

Kiddle: Bow (Weapon) Facts for Kids
    https://kids.kiddle.co/Bow_(weapon)

Murray, Julie. *Archery*. Minneapolis: Abdo, 2023.

Omoth, Tyler. *Bowhunting*. Lake Elmo, MN, Focus Readers, 2018.

Rookie Road: Archery
    https://www.rookieroad.com/archery

Index

Photo Acknowledgments

Image credits: p. 5; Jeff Feverston/Shutterstock, p.6; Steve Oehlenschlager/Shutterstock, p.7; Dimitrii Pichugin/Dreamstime, p.8; nuengbk/Shutterstock, p. 9; ZoranOrcik/Shutterstock, p.10; Anteroxx/Dreamstime, p.11; ramlight/123RF, p.12; Jeffrey B Banke/Shutterstock, p.13; SmLyubov/Shutterstock, p.15; Antonio Gavante/Shutterstock, p 16; ElvK/Shutterstock, p. 17; APN Photography/Shutterstock, p. 18; Aleksey Matrenin/Shutterstock, p. 19; scharfsinn/Shutterstock, p.21; Crystal Mage/Shutterstock, pp. 22-23; MM.Wildlifephotos/Shutterstock, p. 23; Goat and Hare Photography/Shutterstock, p. 24; Geoffrey Kuchera/Shutterstock, p. 25; Edgar G. Biehle/Shutterstock, p. 27; ALEX_UGALEK/Shutterstock, p. 28; Christopher Seno/Shutterstock, p. 29; Jeffrey B.Banke/Shutterstock.

Cover: Nathan Allred/Dreamstime.